Echoes of the Heart

By

Ernest L. Brown

Genre: Inspirational / Spiritual / Self-Help

Format: Paperback, eBook

ISBN: 978-1-971141-49-7

Publisher: Columbus Book Publishers

Publication Date: 02-26-2026

Dedication

I dedicate this book to the loving memory of my mother. She taught our family what real love is. She taught us that a mother's love for her child is greater than any love in the world. I can understand why some mothers do some of the things they do; it's not always because they want to, but because there's a child who needs their support. So, a mother does what she has to do in order to provide for her child. But as long as you look up to God, He will make a way for you. Trust and believe in God, and watch Him come through for you every time. That's called unconditional love. My mother is not here anymore, but I thank God for every day that I had her in this world with me. She may be gone, but all of her love is still here with each and every one of her children. Ella M. Brown, you are my mother for life, and my love for you will last forever.

Acknowledgments

I am deeply grateful to my family, friends, and spiritual mentors, who have supported me throughout my life and writing journey. Special thanks to Joyce Myrick Brown, whose creative direction and encouragement helped bring this book to life. To every reader: thank you for opening your heart to these words. May God bless you abundantly as you walk in faith.

About the Author

Ernest L. Brown is a passionate writer, speaker, and minister whose journey of faith and resilience shapes every word of his work. Growing up in a large, loving family—one of nine children in his mother's home and four more in his father's—Ernest experienced first-hand the joys and struggles that come with a close-knit, extended family. These life experiences, along with witnessing the challenges faced by others, have given him a deep understanding and empathy for people from all walks of life.

Through many seasons of hardship and hope, Ernest gave his life to God and now serves alongside his wife, Apostle Joyce Myrick Brown, as a Minister. Together, they share their home—and hearts—with their beloved Maltese Shih Tzu mix, Bubbles. Ernest is currently pursuing ministerial studies at Kingdom Life Ministries Bible Institute, working toward a degree in Ministry, further deepening his commitment to serving others.

In addition to Echoes of the Heart, Ernest is the author of Words From the Heart and the children's book My Dog Bubbles, with more titles planned in an upcoming series. His writing is rooted in real-life experiences, faith, and a desire to encourage, uplift, and remind every reader that their life has meaning and purpose.

Foreword

In a world filled with uncertainty and change, faith remains our anchor. The journey that led to this book was not a straight path, but one marked by trials, transformation, and moments of deep reflection. Each page is a testament to the power of hope, the necessity of perseverance, and the healing that comes from trusting in God's promises. As you read these reflections, know that they were born from real experiences—days when life felt heavy, and nights when hope seemed distant. Through it all, I discovered that God's love is constant, and His grace is new every morning. The words within these chapters are not just encouragement for others, but reminders to me that every challenge is an opportunity for growth, and every setback is a setup for a greater comeback. This book is an invitation: to pause, to reflect, and to embrace the truth that you are never alone. Whether you are seeking comfort, inspiration, or simply a daily word to lift your spirit, may these echoes of the heart remind you of your worth and the divine purpose woven into your life. I pray that as you journey through these pages, you find strength for today, hope for tomorrow, and peace for your soul. May you be encouraged to persevere, to love deeply, and to trust that God is working all things together for your good.

With gratitude and faith,

Ernest L. Brown

Preface

This introduction sheds light on the motivation and intent behind Echoes of the Heart by E. L. Brown, welcoming you to embark on a journey of encouragement and faith.

Echoes of the Heart is a heartfelt collection of reflections, affirmations, and spiritual encouragement designed to uplift readers through every season of life. Drawing from personal experiences and faith, Ernest L. Brown offers daily inspiration, practical wisdom, and reminders of divine purpose. Each section guides readers through themes of perseverance, hope, healing, relationships, and gratitude, anchored by scripture and real-life stories.

What makes this book unique is the authenticity and empathy woven into every page.

Ernest L. Brown grew up in a large, loving family—one of nine children in his mother's home and four more in his father's—experiencing first-hand the joys and struggles that come with a close-knit, extended family. Through many seasons of hardship and hope, Ernest L. Brown witnessed the challenges faced by others and himself, giving him a deep understanding of the human spirit. His journey led him to give his life to God, and now he serves alongside his wife, Apostle Joyce Myrick Brown, as a Minister. Together, they share their home—and hearts—with their beloved Maltese Shih Tzu mix, Bubbles. Ernest L. Brown is currently pursuing ministerial studies at Kingdom Life Ministries Bible Institute, working toward a degree in Ministry, further deepening his commitment to serving others.

This book is more than a collection of words—it is a companion for every season of life.

Whether you are seeking comfort, motivation, or a daily word to brighten your soul, Echoes of the Heart will meet you where you are and walk with you toward a brighter tomorrow. The reflections and affirmations are rooted in real-life experiences, faith, and a desire to encourage, uplift, and remind every reader that their life has meaning and purpose.

Step into these pages and discover:

- Strength when days feel heavy and hope seems distant
- The power of unconditional love and emotional legacy
- Freedom from the chains of the past and boldness for new beginnings
- The importance of cherishing each moment, nurturing your mind, and cultivating gratitude
- The reminder that you matter, you are loved, and your life has divine purpose

Let these echoes lift your spirit, ignite your dreams, and encourage you to keep moving forward. Ernest L. Brown is also the author of the children's book My Dog Bubbles, with more titles planned in an upcoming series. His writing is an invitation to pause, reflect, and embrace the truth that you are never alone.

Open your heart. Embrace your purpose. Live inspired.

Introduction

This book aims to reach the soul of any person in need of encouragement or motivation, with a positive word for the day. People everywhere, going through different situations, really need an encouraging word—a word, just to tell them that although life may serve them a fast or curveball, they shouldn't give up. To say to them, You can still turn things around, and that if they have fallen someplace in life, they can pick themselves up and make it work. God has not given up on them.

Despite how hard life can seem sometimes, and although some of us find ourselves facing one hurdle after another, life can still be sweet. We can expect hope and a brighter day. We just need someone who cares to be the voice that inspires us and reminds us of that.

I believe I'm one of those voices. I'm the voice for those our Heavenly Father has sent me to. Only He knows what His people need. Only He knows our souls' desires, and only He knows what he has entrusted to me for your benefit. I thank Him for taking my experiences and turning them around for my good; I thank Him for taking what could have been wrong and making it productive.

He made it work out for me so that I would care enough for others, and deposit what I know in you for your good. I know first-hand that every life has a purpose, and that everything works well when it's in its place. In other words, every human being has a purpose, and will become productive once they find theirs. This is all for the glory of the one who gave us life and a purpose.

It is such an honor to serve each of you with a daily word—a word to inspire and motivate you never to give up, and a message to encourage you to keep your head up high and to trust God with the destiny of your life.

Table of Contents

Dedication i

Acknowledgments ii

About the Author iii

Foreword iv

Preface v

Introduction vii

Part I: Foundations of Faith & Identity 1

Section I: A Day in the Real World 2

Enduring with God's Presence 2

Section II: You Matter! 4

Embracing Divine Worth 4

Section III: Keep It Real! — Living Authentically 6

Life is BEAUTIFUL, so don't let it pass you by. 6

Section IV: Never Be Ashamed of Yourself 7

Celebrating Your Journey 7

Section V: Love That Lingers 8

Unconditional Love and Emotional Legacy 8

Part II: Hope, Perseverance & Renewal 10

Section I: Keep Hope About Living 11

Fueling Perseverance 11

Section II: Tomorrow's Not Promised 12

Cherishing Each Day 12

Section III: Don't Give Up! — Holding On Through Trials 14

Section IV: Nothing Stays the Same 16

Welcoming Change 16

Section V: This Is A New Day! 18

Embracing New Beginnings 18

Part III: Healing, Boundaries & Self-Care 21

Section I: Stop the Abuse — Respecting Yourself & Others 22

Section II: Loving Life! 24

Choosing Joy Daily 24

Section III: Take Care of Your Mind! 26

Nurturing Mental Wellness 26

Section IV: The Chains Are Broken 28

Freedom from the Past 28

Part IV: Relationships, Influence & Purpose 31

Section I: Know Who You're Following 32

Choosing Wise Connections 32

Section II: You Can Create It! 34

Turning Dreams into Reality 34

Section III: Thinking Back on Life & Counting My Blessings! 36

Reflecting on Gratitude 36

Section IV: Sitting Back and Giving Thought 40

Intentional Living 40

Part V: Prayer, Patience & Attitude 43

Section I: You're in My Prayers — The Power of Intercession 44

Section II: Don't Rush! — Practicing Patience 45

Section III: Attitude Matters 47

Cultivating a Positive Outlook 47

Closing Reflection: The Heart's Echo 53

Part I: Foundations of Faith & Identity

Section I: A Day in the Real World

Enduring with God's Presence

I made it through another day, thanks to God. I'm happy for every day that I get to see, no matter what may be going on in my life, because life goes on with or without us. Always try to make the best of it. Today may seem like it's more than you can deal with, but that's okay—you can feel that way at times. Just don't stay there. Pick up the pieces and keep looking ahead, because as long as you don't give up on yourself, you'll find the world has so much to offer. You must take the time to find out what it is you want to do. Then, put your all into it.

I know that today may be one of those days when you may want to give up, but don't ever do that. If you weren't meant to be here, God would have taken you away a long time ago. Just brush off that thought, hold your head up, and take a deep breath.

Sometimes, some of us don't want to take the time to do what's best for us. Let's think smarter than that. I love you, and I know that you can do whatever you set your mind to do. Don't worry; God's got you.

Sit back for a moment and give yourself some time. Sitting here and looking at life for what it is, one thing that I know for sure when it comes to anything you want in this world is that if you don't try to get it, you'll only ever want to have it. Whatever you do, don't lose your cool. You will shine again to celebrate another day in the real world!

Message: Every day is a gift, even when it feels heavy. God walks with us through every challenge. If you're facing a tough moment, remember: it's not your final chapter. God's grace is new every morning. Take a deep breath, pick up the pieces, and keep moving. You are here for a reason, and your perseverance is a testimony of faith.

Scripture: "Because of the Lord's great love we are not consumed, for his compassions never fail. They are new every morning; great is your faithfulness."—Lamentations 3:22-23 (NIV)

Reflection: There are days when life feels overwhelming, and giving up seems easier than pressing on. I've had those moments myself. But I've learned that God's purpose for us is not finished. When we trust in His plan and hold our heads high, we discover the strength we didn't know we had. Each day survived is a victory, and each challenge faced is a step forward in faith.

Call to Action: Pause today and thank God for bringing you through another day. Reach out and encourage someone else who may be struggling. Your words and actions can be the hope someone needs.

Affirmation: I am never alone—God's mercy meets me every morning.

Section II: You Matter!

Embracing Divine Worth

I thank God for another day with my life, my right mind, and my health. Most of all, I thank God that He gave me the heart to love people of not just one color, but all colors; not for what they have, but for what He has given me for those He places in my company. A word from the heart! An expression of assurance, hope, and love. We all need someone in life to love us. God will love you for life, even when everyone else has given up on you.

There are so many people in this world who think they don't matter, but let me tell you: you matter so much more than you could ever know. You are so precious, and God has made you unique in your own way.

Just think, some people have everything that they want in this life—anything that money can buy—but when they go home, there's no one there to talk to, or to hold. It's just you and your thoughts, which can sometimes get the best of you. You matter, and those who are a part of your life matter. Always treasure those who want to be in your life, especially if they are there for the right reason.

Again, always remember to thank God for another day of life. Thank Him for your being in your right mind, and for your health. Be grateful for having a heart that loves everyone. We all need love, and even if others give up, remember God will always care about you because you matter.

Message: You are not an accident or an afterthought. God created you with intention and purpose. No matter what others say or how you feel, your life is precious and irreplaceable. The world may overlook you, but God never does. Your presence brings light to those around you, and your uniqueness is a gift.

Scripture: "For you created my inmost being; you knit me together in my mother's womb. I praise you because I am fearfully and wonderfully made; your works are wonderful, I know that full well." — Psalm 139:13-14 (NIV)

Reflection: There have been times when I questioned my worth, wondering if I truly mattered. In those moments, I found comfort in knowing that God sees me, knows me, and loves me beyond measure. Each day, I strive to remember that my value isn't determined by achievements or the opinions of others, but by the love of the One who made me.

Call to Action: Reach out to someone who may feel unseen or undervalued today. Remind them of their worth with a kind word or gesture. Let your actions reflect the love and value God places on every person.

Affirmation: I am valued, loved, and created for a purpose.

Section III: Keep It Real! — Living Authentically

Life is BEAUTIFUL, so don't let it pass you by.

Keep doing your best; even if not for you, do it for your family. Most of us have families at home, and they need our support. Not just financially, but also for compliments, someone to vent to, a shoulder they can cry on, or someone who will be there for them when something in life goes wrong. Together, you can help them fix it. Sometimes the right decision is difficult, especially when it may involve others. Think about it, pray about it, but always be real to your heart, and your mind will rest. Whatever you do in this life, always keep it real.

Message: Life is beautiful, but it's easy to lose sight of that when we're not true to ourselves or those we love. Real support isn't just financial—it's being present, offering encouragement, and sharing honest moments. When you act from the heart, you create a foundation of trust and love that lasts.

Scripture: "Let love be genuine. Abhor what is evil; hold fast to what is good." — Romans 12:9 (ESV)

Reflection: I've learned that the hardest decisions are often the ones that require honesty—with ourselves and with others. When I choose to be real, even when it's uncomfortable, I find peace and clarity. My relationships grow stronger, and my mind can rest knowing I've acted with integrity.

Call to Action: Today, identify one area in your life where you can be more authentic. Whether it's a conversation, a decision, or an act of kindness, let your actions reflect your true self.

Affirmation: I am honest, authentic, and at peace with who I am.

Section IV: Never Be Ashamed of Yourself

Celebrating Your Journey

Be proud of who you are, no matter what someone else may think about you. God put you here to do work. Never worry about what other people say about you. We all have made mistakes in our lives, but you should never let anything stop you from reaching for your star. I believe in you. Believe in yourself and never be ashamed of who you are. Friends for life, but I love you forever.

Message: No one is perfect, and everyone has made mistakes. What matters is how you rise, learn, and move forward. God placed you here for a purpose, and your uniqueness is a gift to the world. Don't let the opinions of others or past failures hold you back from reaching for your dreams.

Scripture: "Therefore, there is now no condemnation for those who are in Christ Jesus." — Romans 8:1 (NIV)

Reflection: I've spent seasons worrying about what others thought of me, letting shame and regret cloud my vision. But I discovered freedom in accepting myself and trusting God's plan. Each day is a new chance to walk boldly and celebrate who I am.

Call to Action: Today, write down one thing you're proud of about yourself. Remind yourself that your journey is valuable, and encourage someone else to do the same.

Affirmation: I am proud of who I am, and I walk forward with confidence and grace.

Section V: Love That Lingers

Unconditional Love and Emotional Legacy

Never regret the love you give.

Message: Love is never wasted. Even when it's not returned in the moment, it plants seeds that bloom in seasons yet to come. Never regret the love you give—it will find its way back to you, transformed, multiplied, and wrapped in grace.

Scripture: Galatians 6:9 (KJV) "Let us not be weary in well doing: for in due season we shall reap, if we faint not."

Reflection: There have been times when I questioned whether my love and kindness made a difference, especially when it wasn't reciprocated. But I've learned that every act of love is a seed sown for a future harvest. Sometimes, the impact of our love isn't seen right away, but it grows quietly, touching lives in ways we may never know. The legacy of love endures beyond moments and memories—it shapes hearts and inspires hope.

Call to Action: Today, choose to love without regret. Reach out to someone who may need encouragement, even if you're unsure how it will be received. Trust that your kindness will make a difference, and let your actions reflect the unconditional love that has been given to you.

Affirmation: I give love freely, knowing it will return to me in unexpected and beautiful ways.

Transition: After embracing authenticity, let's turn our focus to hope—the fuel that keeps us moving forward, even when life feels uncertain.

Part II: Hope, Perseverance & Renewal

Section I: Keep Hope About Living

Fueling Perseverance

Hope is the heartbeat of perseverance.

We made it through another night, so let's start today without excuses.

Message: We made it through another night, so let's start today without excuses. If you're off track, now is the time to correct your course. Life isn't always as difficult as it seems—focus on what makes you happy while handling your responsibilities. Success takes effort, and though it's not always fair or easy, staying hopeful and giving your best will pay off.

Scripture: "Let us hold unswervingly to the hope we profess, for he who promised is faithful." — Hebrews 10:23 (NIV)

Reflection: There have been mornings when I wondered if hope was enough to carry me through. But each time I chose hope over despair, I found new strength and unexpected opportunities. Hope doesn't erase challenges, but it gives us the courage to face them and the faith to believe in better days.

Call to Action: Today, write down one thing you're hopeful for, no matter how small. Let that hope guide your actions and decisions. Share your hope with someone who may need encouragement.

Affirmation: My hope is alive, and I am moving forward with faith.

If you're thankful, show it.

Section II: Tomorrow's Not Promised

Cherishing Each Day

Live fully in the present, for each day is a gift.

Tomorrow is not promised to us. I know that we may not be here tomorrow. It's not promised to me. But if I make it through tonight, I will be better than the day before. I grow more and more each day. Slow down a little so that you can enjoy your life more day by day!

The world has enough problems already; let's not be a part of the problem.

Let's be kind to ourselves and to others. Remember, you teach people how to treat you by letting them know the things that you won't put up with, and meaning it from the heart. You must keep it real; if you don't, it will catch up with you. That's real life. Always remember, tomorrow is not promised to us.

Message: We may not be here tomorrow, and that's a truth we all must face. But if we make it through tonight, we have the chance to grow and become better than we were yesterday. Life is precious—slow down and savor it, day by day. The world has enough problems; let's choose kindness and be part of the solution.

Scripture: "Do not boast about tomorrow, for you do not know what a day may bring." — Proverbs 27:1 (NIV)

Reflection: There have been times when I rushed through life, always planning for tomorrow and missing the beauty of today. I've learned that the present moment is where life happens. By appreciating today, I find peace and gratitude, no matter what tomorrow may hold.

Call to Action: Take time today to slow down and appreciate something simple—a conversation, a meal, a quiet moment. Practice kindness toward yourself and others, knowing that each day is a blessing.

Affirmation: I cherish today and embrace each moment as a gift.

Transition: After reflecting on the uncertainty of tomorrow, let's focus on perseverance and the power of holding on through life's toughest moments.

Section III: Don't Give Up! — Holding On Through Trials

Perseverance is faith in motion.

Don't give up

I know that some people have it hard in this world, but I am telling you to hold on and not give up. I know one thing, even if I don't know anything else: I know that God will answer your prayers. Just believe in yourself. Every day we wake up to a new day, new strength, and another chance to get something right that we may have fallen short in doing the day before.

Thank God for genuine love, for being loved, and for giving it. Thank Him for the love that money can't buy. I pray, God, if I am wrong, that you correct me. If I am lost, guide me—and if I ever start to give up, keep me going, because things change all the time.

With God, you will always come out with what's best for you, even if it's not what you want. God always gives you what you need. Pay attention, and you will see so many things that you have been missing the whole time. We sometimes look for what we want, but not for what we really need.

Message: Life can be hard, and sometimes the weight of your struggles feels unbearable. But even in your darkest moments, remember that God hears your prayers and sees your efforts. Every new day is a chance to try again, to grow stronger, and to experience the love that only God can give. Don't let setbacks define you—let them refine you.

Scripture: "Let us not become weary in doing good, for at the proper time we will reap a harvest if we do not give up." — Galatians 6:9 (NIV)

Reflection: There have been times when I wanted to throw in the towel, convinced that things would never change. But each time I chose to keep going, I discovered new strength and unexpected blessings. God's answers may not always come in the way or timing we expect, but He always provides what we truly need.

Call to Action: Today, take one small step forward, even if it feels difficult. Reach out for support if you need it, and offer encouragement to someone else who may be struggling.

Affirmation: I am resilient, I am hopeful, and I will not give up.

Transition: After persevering through life's challenges, it's vital to recognize the importance of self-worth and healthy boundaries.

Section IV: Nothing Stays the Same

Welcoming Change

Change is inevitable—growth is a choice. Nothing stays the same.

The phrase for today is "nothing stays the same;" it either gets better or worse. But the good thing is you get to choose because it's your life. It's easy to plan, but making the right decision is what counts. What matters is how you may respond to a situation. Always keep your head up, no matter what's going on in your life. God has made you wonderful and has already put the strength in you to overcome any situation that is going to come our way.

We will have both good and bad circumstances and situations in life; this is just part of growing up from a child to an adult. Remember this: you hold the key to your destiny. All the things that you could ever want in this lifetime, you can have. You can have them all, but you must stay focused on you and not anyone else. You can watch others, but do not follow them. Stay on your path because God has already made it for you Himself.

Message: Life is always moving, and nothing stays the same forever. Circumstances may get better or worse, but you have the power to choose your response. God has given you strength and wisdom to face whatever comes your way. Focus on your own journey, and trust that your path is uniquely designed for you.

Scripture: "See, I am doing a new thing! Now it springs up; do you not perceive it? I am making a way in the wilderness and streams in the wasteland." — Isaiah 43:19 (NIV)

Reflection: I've seen seasons of both joy and hardship, and I've learned that change can be a blessing in disguise. When I stopped resisting and started embracing the lessons each change brought, I found new opportunities for growth and gratitude. Staying focused on my own path helped me discover my true purpose.

Call to Action: Today, reflect on an area of your life that is changing. Instead of fearing the unknown, ask God to show you the opportunity within the change. Write down one positive thing that could come from this new season.

Affirmation: I welcome change, knowing it leads me to growth and new beginnings.

Section V: This Is A New Day!

Embracing New Beginnings

This is a new day, and I am so glad to be alive. It's a blessing from God, and I can't thank Him enough. My life has been the way I made it, and I'm trying to correct it. But I know, with the hand of God on me, and with Him seeing my heart, He will help me to straighten things out. We're all blessed. We just take different turns in life. We all want to get back on track, and if we're alive, we can do that. God is not going to turn His back on us.

We all need somebody in our lives. No matter what anybody says or feels, even if they say that they don't need anybody, that's not true. We all need somebody in our lives, for one reason or another. Don't ever think that you can walk alone because you can't. We all need somebody for something... Anything that you want to do in this world, trust me, it's in you to do it. There are a lot of people out there with a lot of knowledge in their heads, but they let it go to waste.

Don't ever let life pass you by like that. You were put here for a reason, and it wasn't for anything bad. There's always a good reason why someone falls into the world. That's why we learn things. We have to learn things from people. However, we need to learn from the right people—not just from anybody who's just saying what you want to hear, but someone who will tell you the truth. The truth is what makes you successful in this world.

You've got to be honest, you've got to be straight, and you've got to know what you're doing. You've got to go for what you really want, not what you think you want. Because life doesn't give you a second chance. Only God gives you that.

In reality, you know, when chance passes you by, it doesn't usually come back and get you. Think smart. Make wise decisions and make good moves in life, and you'll win every time. The key to life is to have patience and make time; it takes time to do things. Too many people don't have time.

Slow down. There's enough time. There are twenty-four hours in a day, whether they move quickly or slowly; no more, no less. Just hold on and keep your head up. When it's raining, you still have to keep your head up because you want to see where you're going.

Do the same thing when the storm comes your way. When things aren't working out your way, keep your head up; it's going to get better. You have to believe in yourself, even if no one else believes in you. Always believe in yourself. I love you for life!

Part III: Healing, Boundaries & Self-Care

Section I: Stop the Abuse — Respecting Yourself & Others

We have all, in some form or fashion, been abused. It's not always physical abuse that harms you. It can be the way someone talks to you, or the way they may ignore you. Abuse comes in such a wide variety. So be careful, and always keep an open mind. Listen to understand, not just to respond.

Love yourself enough to keep it real with yourself. That's called living in real life. Know your worth and let no one tell you differently. God has made you in a particular way, and there is no one else like you. That's what separates you from the rest of the world. Stay positive and keep it moving. You can do it. Stop the abuse. "I give thanks to you, for I am created with awe and wonder; your deeds are extraordinary, and my soul understands this completely." – Psalm 139:14, (NIV)

Message: Abuse isn't always physical—it can be emotional, verbal, or even the silent treatment. No matter the form, it leaves marks on the heart and mind. You are worthy of kindness, respect, and love. God made you unique, and no one has the right to diminish your value. Stand firm in your worth and refuse to accept mistreatment from anyone.

Scripture: "The Lord is close to the brokenhearted and saves those who are crushed in spirit." — Psalm 34:18 (NIV)

Reflection: I've seen how words and actions can wound deeper than any physical blow. It took time to realize that healing begins with self-respect and the courage to set boundaries. When I started loving myself enough to say "no" to abuse, I discovered a new freedom and peace.

Call to Action: Today, reflect on your relationships and interactions. If something or someone is causing you harm, take a step to protect yourself—whether it's speaking up, seeking help, or simply walking away. You deserve to be treated with dignity.

Affirmation: I am worthy of love, respect, and kindness.

Section II: Loving Life!

Choosing Joy Daily

I love every minute of my life, no matter what's going on. Straight talk. Treasure every day that you get to see, cherish every breath that you get to take, treasure everyone that you have in your life who loves you, and treasure every step that you get to make, because one day it all will come to an end. True talk.

One important thing about your life is that you have to choose how it goes. Be sure to always think before making any kind of decision, because life only comes around once. So, always be at your best, no matter what you do. God has made you so precious, and you are a diamond. Just look in the mirror and see how beautiful you really are.

I love you, and I don't even know you. That's because I know that you are beautiful on the inside. Because God never made anything that wasn't perfect. I thank God for my being here today, with my health and my strength, and I will never take anything that I have in my life for granted. I have messed up in life so many times, but now I am on the right track, and I won't look back at my mistakes. They are behind me, and my life has changed for the better. Thank God for the mercy that He has shown me.

Message: Choose joy daily, no matter your circumstances. Treasure every moment, every breath, and every person who loves you. Life is precious and unique, and you are a diamond—beautiful inside and out.

Scripture: "I give thanks to you, for I am created with awe and wonder; your deeds are extraordinary, and my soul understands this completely." – Psalm 139:14 (NIV)

Reflection: I have messed up in life so many times, but now I am on the right track, and I won't look back at my mistakes. They are behind me, and my life has changed for the better. Thank God for the mercy that He has shown me.

Call to Action: Treasure every day, every breath, and every person who loves you. Make thoughtful decisions and always strive to be your best, knowing that life only comes around once.

Affirmation: I love every minute of my life, and I am thankful for the mercy and strength God gives me each day.

Section III: Take Care of Your Mind!

Nurturing Mental Wellness

…And always remember this:

- If you're thankful, show it.
- If you love someone, tell them.
- If you're wrong, fess up.
- If you are confused, ask questions.
- If you learn something, teach others.
- If you're stuck, ask for help.
- If you made a mistake, apologize.
- If you stumble or trip, get back up.
- If someone needs help, help them.
- If you see wrong, take a stance.

In all things, whatever may go on in a day, if you take care of your mind, your mind will take care of your body. True talk!

Message: Your mind is the foundation of your well-being. Nurture it with gratitude, honesty, curiosity, and kindness. Every day offers opportunities to learn, grow, and help others. When you care for your mind, you empower your body and spirit to thrive.

Scripture: "Do not conform to the pattern of this world, but be transformed by the renewing of your mind." — Romans 12:2 (NIV)

Reflection: There are days when my mind feels overwhelmed by worries, mistakes, or confusion. But I've learned that asking for help, admitting when I'm wrong, and sharing what I learn brings clarity and peace. Taking care of my mind is an act of self-love and a gift to those around me.

Call to Action: Today, choose one way to nurture your mental wellness—express gratitude, ask for help if you need it, or offer support to someone else. Remember, small actions can make a big difference in your mental health.

Affirmation: I honor my mind by caring for it daily. I am open to learning, growing, and healing.

Section IV: The Chains Are Broken

Freedom from the Past

This morning, I woke up feeling weighed down by worries and stress as though I was bound in chains. As I prayed, I realized that God had already set me free from these burdens long ago. I simply needed to let go and trust in His deliverance. I looked up to Heaven, and I realized that my chains broke many generations ago, and all I had to do was take them off.

So many people will try to make you feel like you are still limited in what you can do and how far you can go in life, but no one knows your limits except you and God. If you can think of it, you can do it. Some things may take more time than others, but it will be worth it for you. I had to take my time and take the chains off me. Now take them off of you.

Mark 5:8, Acts 16:23-26, Psalm 116:16, and Psalm 107:13-16.

Message: Freedom from the past is possible when you trust in God's deliverance. The burdens you carry are not meant to define you—God has already broken those chains. Let go, believe in your worth, and step into the future He has prepared for you.

Scripture: "The Lord is close to the brokenhearted and saves those who are crushed in spirit." — Psalm 34:18 (NIV) (Also referenced: Mark 5:8, Acts 16:23-26, Psalm 116:16, Psalm 107:13-16)

Reflection: There are days when the weight of past mistakes and worries feels overwhelming, but I've learned that God's grace is greater than any chain that binds me. When I choose to let go and trust in His love, I find freedom and peace. The journey may take time, but every step forward is a victory.

Call to Action: Today, reflect on what may be holding you back. Pray for strength to let go of past burdens and trust that God has already set you free. Encourage someone else who may feel trapped by their past—remind them that freedom is possible.

Affirmation: I am free from the chains of my past. God's grace has set me free, and I walk forward in hope and strength.

Part IV:

Relationships, Influence & Purpose

Section I: Know Who You're Following

Choosing Wise Connections

The word for today: "Always stay connected with someone who knows where they are going in life." If you're following anyone for any other reason, it will be just like following a blind man who doesn't know where he is supposed to go. If you are going to follow anyone, make sure that you know who you are following.

Not everyone knows where they're going. Some people are just as lost as we are sometimes. That's why I encourage you to always think before you make any kind of move. Let God direct your path. He's never wrong. Keep the faith in yourself, and in Him.

Man will sometimes get off track, but not always intentionally. But we as people can only do so much before God steps in to finish whatever it is that we couldn't do, just like your parents, who took care of the things that you couldn't take care of as a child. So, whatever it is that you even think you are going through, give it to God and leave it there at His feet. He's got it from there; He doesn't need your help.

Message: Choose your connections wisely. Not everyone knows where they are going, and following the wrong person can lead you astray. Seek out those who have vision, integrity, and faith. Let God direct your path, and trust that He will place the right people in your life for your growth and purpose.

Scripture: "Walk with the wise and become wise, for a companion of fools suffers harm." — Proverbs 13:20 (NIV)

Reflection: There have been times when I followed others without considering where they were headed, only to find myself lost or off track. I've learned that wisdom comes from being intentional about who I allow to influence me. When I let God guide my relationships, I find clarity, support, and encouragement to pursue my purpose.

Call to Action: Today, reflect on the people you follow or look up to. Are they leading you closer to your goals and values? Pray for discernment and courage to connect with those who inspire you to grow and live with purpose.

Affirmation: I choose my connections wisely. God directs my path, and I am surrounded by people who encourage and uplift me.

Section II: You Can Create It!

Turning Dreams into Reality

Word for today: "Sometimes God will change your circle to change your life." True talk. Regardless of your current circumstances, if you can imagine something better for yourself, you can create it. I once heard something like this:

- Write out your dreams.

- Your written dreams become your goals.

- Your goals, broken down, become your plans in life.

- Your plans, with determination, become your reality. So, what are you going to do now?

- Your mind is so great—just use it. True talk.

Message: You have the power to turn your dreams into reality. No matter your circumstances, if you can envision something better for yourself, you can take steps to achieve it. God may change your circle to help you grow—embrace new opportunities and trust in your ability to create the life you desire.

Scripture: "Commit to the Lord whatever you do, and he will establish your plans." — Proverbs 16:3 (NIV)

Reflection: There have been times when I doubted my ability to change my life, but writing down my dreams and breaking them into actionable steps helped me move forward. Determination and faith are key—sometimes God shifts our relationships and environment to help us reach our goals.

Call to Action: Today, write out your dreams and break them down into goals and plans. Take one step toward making your dreams a reality, and trust that God is guiding your journey.

Affirmation: I am a creator of my destiny. With faith, determination, and action, I turn my dreams into reality.

Section III: Thinking Back on Life & Counting My Blessings!

Reflecting on Gratitude

I count my blessings every day—especially the ones that we often call little. They sometimes mean the most. I remember when I was just about ten years old; there were nine of us children, and we didn't have the things that we wanted to have because my mother had to do her best to make sure that we had food to eat. She had no help raising us. She did her best, and for all of the things that we could not afford, she made up for it with all of the love she had in her heart.

That was worth more than anything that money could ever buy. Every day when I get up, I know that it's a blessing. God has been and still is good to me. I could never thank Him enough.

I still remember those days. We didn't have a lot in the house to eat, but my mama still made sure that we ate first. Whatever we didn't eat, that's what she ate.

Being so young, I didn't realize at first what was going on, but as I got older, I saw just what she was doing. She had a heart of gold. I think that we, as parents, uncles, aunts, and other members of the extended family, have to uphold each other.

We've got to stick together, whether we have something or not. I'm very thankful and blessed because we made it. We are here today because of prayers. My mama prayed a lot. She believed in God, and so do I. I will never tell anybody I don't believe in God. I've seen the things that He has done for me; things that no other man could have done. Every day I'm blessed, and I count my blessings. I'm very thankful! I don't always look for big things to be blessed, but little things that we keep overlooking; that's what counts the most.

Always try to be kind to others because everybody needs somebody to be kind to them. Even you and me. I love everybody, but that doesn't mean you have to hang out with everybody. Everybody's got different ways. Everyone has a unique path, but with effort, you can achieve your goals—even if it takes time. Just put forth an effort to treat new people with kindness and make a move. Don't be scared. Stepping outside of your comfort zone is essential for personal growth and success. Don't be afraid to try new things and embrace change. True progress happens when you challenge yourself.

Learn how to talk to people. Look them in the eyes when you talk to them, and let them know you are interested in what they are saying. Try to pick a person up sometime when you see them down. Sometimes words mean more than anything in the world.

Your words have power, and you have to use them wisely because you can tear a person down with your mouth and words just as well as build them up. Each of us benefits from encouragement. Daily support helps us grow, and having someone uplift us every day makes a difference. Say something kind to everybody. Most of all, be kind to yourself.

The world was built for love out of the love God has for every one of us. Love is always going to overrule. Two things you can't beat are love and the truth. That's the truth, you know. You just have to take life seriously now because every day is special. You never know when our last day will be.

We have to be more like leaders now; we have to be more of an inspiration. Many of us now have families, and there may be young children present, even if they are not our own. We need to start setting an example for them. We're always telling them what they're doing wrong, but we need to start fixing things so they know what to do right. Some of them just don't know.

We've got people out here who are grown and still don't know what to do because they have never been shown. So, they just follow suit. They get up every day and do whatever they want. Everybody wants something good out of life, but not everyone knows how to get it.

So, when you've got somebody showing you how to get it and how to do it right, take the time out for yourself and get that knowledge. We all need it, and—with the way the world is going now— we will be lost without it. I mean, that's just true talk. We have to pull this thing together now.

There are too many people out here who are smart… to do no good. Come on, now. Don't throw away your blessings. It's a blessing to be talented, and everybody has one. Everybody is special; everybody is worth something. You just have to be in your rightful place. You mean the world. I love you!

Message: Gratitude transforms ordinary moments into blessings. Reflecting on your life and counting your blessings—especially the small ones—brings perspective, joy, and a deeper appreciation for what truly matters.

Scripture: "Give thanks in all circumstances; for this is God's will for you in Christ Jesus." — 1 Thessalonians 5:18 (NIV)

Reflection: Looking back, I realize that the love, prayers, and kindness I received shaped my life far more than material things ever could. The little things—kind words, daily support, and simple acts of love—are what count the most. Gratitude helps me see the beauty in every day and inspires me to be kind to others.

Call to Action: Today, take a moment to count your blessings—big and small. Express gratitude to someone who has made a difference in your life, and offer encouragement to someone who may need it.

Affirmation: I am grateful for every blessing in my life, and I choose to share kindness and encouragement with others.

Section IV: Sitting Back and Giving Thought

Intentional Living

Today is one of those days when I don't have much to do. So I am sitting back, just thinking of all the things I would love to do in this lifetime. But also, I know that the only way I'm going to make it in life is to get up, get dressed, go out into the world, and find my rightful place.

We will never know just what we are made of until our backs are against the wall; then we see how strong we truly are. We all have more strength than we know, but it doesn't show up until it's needed. So, always remember that there are no limits to how far you can go in life if you only come out of your comfort zone. Life is good—just don't be afraid to live it.

Message: Intentional living means taking time to reflect, plan, and act with purpose. When you pause to consider your dreams and strengths, you discover new opportunities for growth and fulfillment. Life is good—don't be afraid to step out and live it fully.

Scripture: "Commit to the Lord whatever you do, and he will establish your plans." — Proverbs 16:3 (NIV)

Reflection: We often don't realize our true strength until we face challenges. Taking time to sit back and give thought to your life helps you recognize your potential and the steps you need to take to reach your goals. Every moment of reflection is a chance to grow.

Call to Action: Today, set aside a quiet moment to reflect on your goals and dreams. Write down one step you can take to move closer to your purpose. Don't be afraid to leave your comfort zone—growth happens when you challenge yourself.

Affirmation: I am intentional in my actions and open to new possibilities. I embrace my strength and step forward with purpose.

Part V: Prayer, Patience & Attitude

Section I: You're in My Prayers — The Power of Intercession

I want you to know that you're in my prayers. Maybe you're overwhelmed because you have been dealing with so much lately; maybe you're wondering about your outcome in life and if things will turn out all right.

I'm here to remind you that, although life brings many changes, God's love for us remains the same. He's always there. He guides us through decisions and helps us do hard things, things we can't do on our own. Remember that your mind is just like a computer, so learn how to use it.

Message: Prayer is a powerful act of love and support. Even when life feels overwhelming, know that you are being lifted up in prayer. God's love is constant, and He is always present to guide, comfort, and strengthen you.

Scripture: "Therefore confess your sins to each other and pray for each other so that you may be healed. The prayer of a righteous person is powerful and effective." — James 5:16 (NIV)

Reflection: There have been times when I felt alone in my struggles, but knowing someone was praying for me brought comfort and hope. Prayer connects us to God and to each other, reminding us that we are never truly alone.

Call to Action: Today, take a moment to pray for someone who may be struggling. Reach out with a word of encouragement or let them know you are thinking of them. Your prayers and kindness can make a difference in someone's life.

Affirmation: I am supported by prayer and surrounded by God's love. My prayers for others are powerful and bring hope and healing.

Section II: Don't Rush! — Practicing Patience

Take your time. There are only twenty-four hours in a day; whether they pass quickly or slowly, you still get 24 hours a day. As spoken in Psalm 127:1-5,

Except the LORD build the house, they labour in vain that build it: except the LORD keep the city, the watchman waketh but in vain.

It is vain for you to rise up early, to sit up late, to eat the bread of sorrows: for so he giveth his beloved sleep.

Lo, children are an heritage of the LORD: and the fruit of the womb is his reward.

As arrows are in the hand of a mighty man, so are children of the youth (KJV).

In other words, just slow down, take your time, and enjoy your life and your family.

Remember: you can't get everything done at once. Pace yourself and keep your focus on God and His will for you.

Message: Patience is a gift we give ourselves and those we love. Life moves at its own pace—there are only twenty-four hours in a day, and we cannot rush what is meant to unfold in its time. When we slow down, we allow ourselves to enjoy our families, appreciate our blessings, and trust that God is working behind the scenes. Remember: you can't get everything done at once. Pace yourself, and keep your focus on God and His will for you.

Scripture: "Except the LORD build the house, they labour in vain that build it: except the LORD keep the city, the watchman waketh but in vain. It is vain for you to rise up early, to sit up late, to eat the bread of sorrows: for so he giveth his beloved sleep." — Psalm 127:1-2 (KJV)

Reflection: There have been times when I tried to force things to happen, believing that my effort alone could shape the outcome. But I learned that true progress comes when I trust God's timing and let go of the need to control every detail. Patience isn't just about waiting—it's about finding peace in the process, knowing that God is building something beautiful in my life, even when I can't see it yet. When I slow down, I discover joy in the present and gratitude for each step along the way.

Call to Action: Today, take a deep breath and give yourself permission to slow down. Make time for what matters most—family, faith, and self-care. Trust that God is guiding your journey, and let go of the pressure to do it all at once. Reach out to someone who may be feeling overwhelmed and remind them that patience is a strength, not a weakness.

Affirmation: I am patient and at peace, trusting God's timing in every area of my life. I embrace each moment, knowing that what is meant for me will come in its perfect time.

Section III: Attitude Matters

Cultivating a Positive Outlook

It's a new day, and I'm here again, alive and well. I give God thanks. It's a day He didn't have to let me see, but His mercy got me here. I just want to say to anybody and everybody that we all go through some changes in life, but we can make it.

You've gone through some worse things in life before, and you made it. You can do it again. Just put all you've got into something. There are no limitations to what you can accomplish in this world. Whatever you do, put your mind to it and go for it. Get that! You can do it—I believe in you; I don't even have to see you to know you can do it, because I know what God put in a person. We have skills, talents, motivations, and dreams, so you can achieve whatever you set out to accomplish.

Some things take time, and you won't get them overnight like that. Anything worth having can be yours through time and work. You need to have patience. Most of all, you need to have the right attitude when walking through life—attitude matters.

You can't just walk through life treating people any kind of way. Some people are extraordinary. When it comes to your life, you hold them. You embrace that person. That could be your key to achieving something in life. When our heads get a little too big, we can act like we don't need certain things and certain people.

Don't ever get too big-headed; you start pushing people away who have been there for you. Life is big. There will be a time when you are going to come back around. Coming back doesn't have to mean you're doing badly; it could be because of a business deal or something else. You might be the key to that person getting what they need, or to where they may need to go. But by the time you get back with them, they'll have cut you loose and moved on, not thinking you would ever need each other again. Stay humble.

Also, don't look for credit when you do something for somebody. Do it from the heart, because God sees what you do, and you will be blessed a hundred-fold. Keep your head up and keep praying; stay on your knees before God. Stop looking for men because they will let you down. Not intentionally all the time, but they are not God. Some things have to be done just between you and God. Take time out for God just like you take time out for all the rest of the stuff you do.

When you go out on the street, you should come back with an excellent report. Don't leave home and come back with a problem you didn't have before. It's not good to go home at night without having benefited from anything while you were out. If you've just created another problem, that's defeating life. You're smarter than that. You should think more wisely than that. Life goes around once, and you can't keep rewinding it. It doesn't work that way. We have to teach others the same thing.

Next, you need to start showing people that you do love them. If you love somebody, show them that you love them. Love is something that everybody has in their heart. The first thing God put in you when you were conceived in your mother was love, because that's what He is. You don't have to teach anybody how to love anybody. You don't have to do that because that is something that's in you. As you get older, the people you love may change, but no one can take away all the love someone has in their heart. Love is something that God planted in you.

Have you noticed it? You can find the worst person in the world, the worst killer, but even he has somebody he loves. You can't erase love from a person's heart. God put that in there. The worst person in the world, a person who nobody wants to deal with, still loves somebody. There's somebody that even he trusts. That's life.

Never mistreat people who place their trust in you. Trust is a favor and favor is worth way more than money. Trust me; it carries further than money. A lot of things can't be bought with cash, but the favor will get it for you. Not having enough money to get you to a destination may be an issue, but support is favor, and it will get you there—somebody may come by and give you a ride to that spot. You might have been there, sitting with money in your pocket. God works things out for you, but you should not take advantage of a situation. Always learn how to display love back. If somebody gives it to you, show that person that you appreciate them.

If you go through some difficult times with a person, don't go squashing their name around just because you all got mad, or because things didn't go the way you wanted them to go with that person. That's only a part of life; you just deal with those things. Work it out—and if you don't work it out, just keep going. But don't destroy a person's name, because you have one, too, and I think you would like for your name to be protected.

But whatever God says you are, that's who you are. Nobody else can tell you who you are. Don't let the enemy tell you that you are not something; if he tells you that you are not something, know that you are. If he says you are something, then know that you are not. The enemy always does the opposite of God; If God says you're special, you're marvelous, the devil tells you you're no good and that you're worthless. That's just the way he works.

Whenever something negative comes to you, turn it around and make it into something positive.

You can do it! It's just like having a bad day. Your day is going badly, but if you had a lot of money in your pocket, it would turn out differently. It's still the same day, but your attitude changed. Why? Because you changed your outlook. The money didn't do it—you did. Your attitude changed towards that day, right after you started receiving things you wanted. You choose to be happy or sad. The choice is yours. Now, what are you going to do?

Message: It's a new day, and I'm here again, alive and well. I give God thanks. It's a day He didn't have to let me see, but His mercy got me here. We all go through changes in life, but we can make it. You've overcome worse before, and you can do it again. There are no limitations to what you can accomplish—put your mind to it and go for it. Attitude matters: how you approach life, treat others, and respond to challenges shapes your journey. Stay humble, show love, and remember that favor and trust carry further than money. Choose to be positive, grateful, and kind.

Scripture: "Whatever you do, work at it with all your heart, as working for the Lord, not for human masters." — Colossians 3:23 (NIV)

(Note: The section references several scriptures about attitude and perseverance; Colossians 3:23 is a fitting complement to the themes expressed.)

Reflection: There have been times when my attitude determined the outcome of my day more than my circumstances. I've learned that patience, humility, and gratitude open doors that force and frustration never could. When I choose to see each day as a gift and treat others with kindness, I find joy and purpose even in difficult moments. The right attitude transforms setbacks into opportunities and relationships into sources of strength. Life is too short to carry negativity—embrace the power of a positive outlook.

Call to Action: Today, make a conscious choice to approach every situation with a positive attitude. Show appreciation to someone who has helped you, and offer encouragement to someone who may be struggling. Practice humility and gratitude, and let your actions reflect the love and favor you wish to receive. If you encounter challenges, pause and ask yourself how a shift in attitude could change the outcome.

Affirmation: I choose a positive attitude, knowing it shapes my life and relationships. I am grateful, humble, and open to the blessings each day brings. With faith and kindness, I overcome challenges and inspire others.

Closing Reflection: The Heart's Echo

The next time I see you, I want to hold you a little longer. I want you to see yourself the way I see you—beautiful, amazing, irreplaceable. I want you to feel my love not just in words, but in presence, in effort, in action. You are everything to me, and I'll never stop reminding you.

Message: The next time I see you, I want to hold you a little longer. I want you to see yourself the way I see you—beautiful, amazing, irreplaceable. I want you to feel my love not just in words, but in presence, in effort, in action. You are everything to me, and I'll never stop reminding you.

Scripture: "Love never gives up, never loses faith, is always hopeful, and endures through every circumstance." — 1 Corinthians 13:7 (NLT)

Reflection: Love is the thread that weaves through every chapter of our lives. It endures through hardships, celebrates our victories, and remains steadfast even when hope feels distant. In moments of doubt or loneliness, remember that you are deeply loved and valued. The echoes of love—spoken and unspoken—shape who we are and remind us that we are never truly alone.

Call to Action: Today, choose one way to nurture your mental wellness—express gratitude, ask for help if you need it, or offer support to someone else. Remember, small actions can make a big difference in your mental health and in the lives of those around you.

Affirmation: I am worthy of love, and I carry its echo in my heart. I choose to give and receive love freely, knowing it endures through every circumstance.

Are you ready to be inspired, uplifted, and reminded of your true worth?

Step into the pages of Echoes of the Heart and discover a journey of hope, healing, and purpose. Through heartfelt reflections, daily affirmations, and real-life stories, Ernest L. Brown invites you to embrace the power of faith and perseverance—no matter where you are on your path.

This is more than a book. It's a companion for every season of life.

- Find strength when days feel heavy and hope seems distant.
- Celebrate your unique journey and the unconditional love that surrounds you.
- Break free from the chains of the past and step boldly into new beginnings.
- Learn to cherish each moment, nurture your mind, and cultivate gratitude.
- Be reminded: You matter, you are loved, and your life has divine purpose.

Let these echoes lift your spirit, ignite your dreams, and encourage you to keep moving forward.

Whether you're seeking comfort, motivation, or a daily word to brighten your soul, Echoes of the Heart will meet you where you are and walk with you toward a brighter tomorrow.

Open your heart. Embrace your purpose. Live inspired.